# WHITEWATER TALES OF TERROR

Copyright © 1983 by William Nealy
All rights reserved
Printed in the United States of America
Published by Menasha Ridge Press
Hillsborough, North Carolina 27278
Second printing, 1985

*Library of Congress Cataloging in Publication Data:*
Nealy, William, 1953–
    Whitewater tales of terror
    1. White-water canoeing—Caricatures and cartoons.
2. American wit and humor, Pictorial.   I. Title.
NC1429.N42A4   1983   741.5′973   83-22051
ISBN 0-89732-024-7

# WHITEWATER TALES OF TERROR,
## DON'T GET OFF THE INTERSTATE

by William Nealy

Menasha Ridge Press
Hillsborough, North Carolina

This book is dedicated to the three Dans...

Big Dan

Young Dan

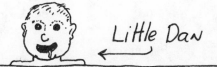

Little Dan

# Acknowledgements....

First of all I'd like to thank a few people for their kind assistance, comic inspiration and psychic life-support... Mark Brown, Tam Fletcher, Tom Love, Holland "Is this _all_?" Wallace, Bob Miller, Cliff and Alice Earle, John Barbour, Don Banducci, Tom Schlinkert, Sarah Crichton, Guy Martin, John Regan, Class VI Riverrunners, Neal & Mothra Allen, Reg Lake, Haze Hanff, John Mills, Ester Szabo, Paul Thompson, Ed Gertler, Thrifty Outfitters, Charlie Walbridge, Terry Curtin, Aqua Pac, David Brown, Louise Nealy, Henry Unger, Bob & Alice Vernon, Friedrich Nietzsche, Bob Sehlinger, Frank Fleming, John Wassen, Tom Kruck, Bob, James & J.T, Bruce Hare, The Doobie Bros. (_Not_ the band!), The Ramones (_The_ band), Jim Perrigo, John Dragon, Mike Kinnard, Edgar Hitchcock, Ron Mace, Joan Wallace, Rangeley & Jim, Tracy Tiller, Barrie Wallace, Jim Screvin, Creative Printers, U-2, James Watt (thanks for the T-shirt royalties, Jim!), Glen Kovac, Doug Bush, Chance Danger, Bruce Tiller....

* Back Cover Photo by Edgar Hitchcock *

Fear of women is the
basis of good health.

Spanish Proverb

# Colorful River Expressions
# #17

"It was so hot.."

# Ask Mr. Manners

**Dear Mr. Manners,**

How long can you legitimately surf a hole before being called a "hole hog" or worse? My paddling buddies say two minutes is the rule. What do you say?

Perplexed

**Dear Perplexed,**

Your buddies are right as long as they're paddling in the Southeast. Out West the general rule is 3 minutes unless you are posing for advertising or magazine photographs, in which case you get an extra minute. In the Mid West there is no time rule, providing you can find a hole to surf.

**Dear Mr. Manners,**

Last weekend I saw this gorgeous chick guiding a raft. I paddled right up and asked her if she wanted to party later on. Here's the unbelievable part; she hammered a 5 gal. bailing bucket over my head, pulled me out of my boat, and 'binered my jock strap to a "D'ring and dragged me through a nasty rapid before letting me go! Chicks tell me I look like Tom Selleck, so what gives?

Frustrated

Dear Frustrated,

Did you forget to mention your "dynamite Colombo"? Consider yourself lucky to be alive. She probably had a negative reaction to your approach, which I gather is none too subtile. Next time pretend you have dislocated your elbow and appeal to her maternal instincts. Keep your mouth shut except to breathe.

Dear Mr. Manners,

If you eddy out in a rapid and find yourself breaking in line to surf a hole do you have to go to the end of the line? Ed (my paddling partner) says you _can_ break in line only during the initial running of the rapid as long as your intent was to eddy out to rest or scout, not to surf. Does Ed's doctrine of malicious intent apply on the river?

Confused in Ohio

Dear Ohio,

Go to the end of the line. Good luck to your buddy Ed.

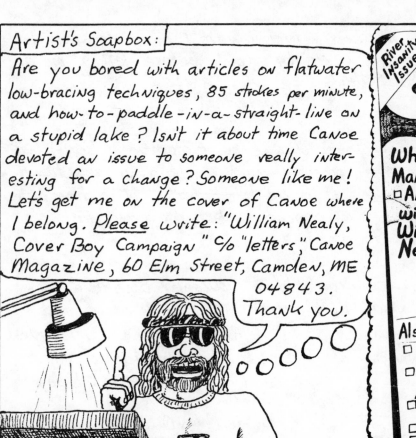

**Artist's Soapbox:**

Are you bored with articles on flatwater low-bracing techniques, 85 strokes per minute, and how-to-paddle-in-a-straight-line on a stupid lake? Isn't it about time Canoe devoted an issue to someone really interesting for a change? Someone like me! Let's get me on the cover of Canoe where I belong. <u>Please</u> write: "William Nealy, Cover Boy Campaign" c/o "letters", Canoe Magazine, 60 Elm Street, Camden, ME 04843. Thank you.

River Insanity Issue!

The Magazine of Self-propelled Water Travel

# Canoe

December 1982

Why Is This Man Smiling? □ An Interview with William Nealy

Also Inside:

□ Women Paddlers: Can't Live With 'Em, Can't Live Without 'Em
□ Zen Shuttle Driving: The Subtile Dance Of Automobiles - An Essay By Master Designer /Philosopher/Guru Mike Ultimate
□ The Love Boat: A Radical New Boat That Strokes You Back!
□ Flatwater Boaters - Wimps or Pinheads?
□ The Romance of Neoprene Booties
□ Smurfs Up! Down a California River With Those Loveable Little Smurfs!
... Plus Lots More!

# A Viable Alternative to Neoprene:

You will need
3,000 medium hamsters
6,400 #2 safety pins
20 lbs Purina Rodent Chow

*It's so warm you'd swear it's alive!*

UNIQUE
Outdoor Equipment

# Winter's Early

## Catalogue Parody

We will engrave your message!

Ach!

# Engraved Sierra Dribble-Cup confuses, humiliates..

Everyone knows at least one complete outdoor nebbish who would covet a gold-plated engraved Sierra cup. You'll enjoy the shocked expression on his or her face when they dump steaming chicken broth down their shirt!

✳8102 Sierra Cup- gold plated....$39.95

# Giant Ionizing Air Cleaner freshens even at high altitude!

Clean air isn't what it used to be in our wilderness areas. The Winter's Early Ionizing Air Cleaner can cycle up to 10,000 cubic feet of air per minute at altitudes up to 20,000.

Ionizing Air Cleaner $1579.00

1,200 Nickel Cadmium "C" cell batteries (6.75ea) $8,100.00

Solar Nicad Charger $695.00

An end to unkempt campsites and overgrown backcountry trails.....the Takedown Weedeater!

Takedown Weedeater with carry case
#1107..........$109.95

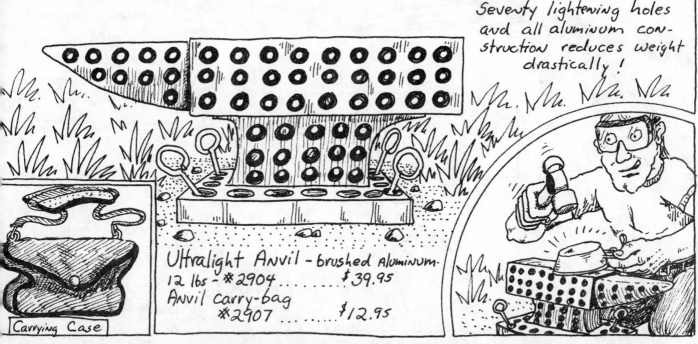

# Ultimate Aerial-Aquatic sport is Not a fad.......Parayakking!

Whether you're a dedicated kayaker, parachutist, or a wealthy moron you'll get a thrill from Parayakking, the new ultimate sport for the '80's!

① ② Quick release for super "Endo" ③ ④

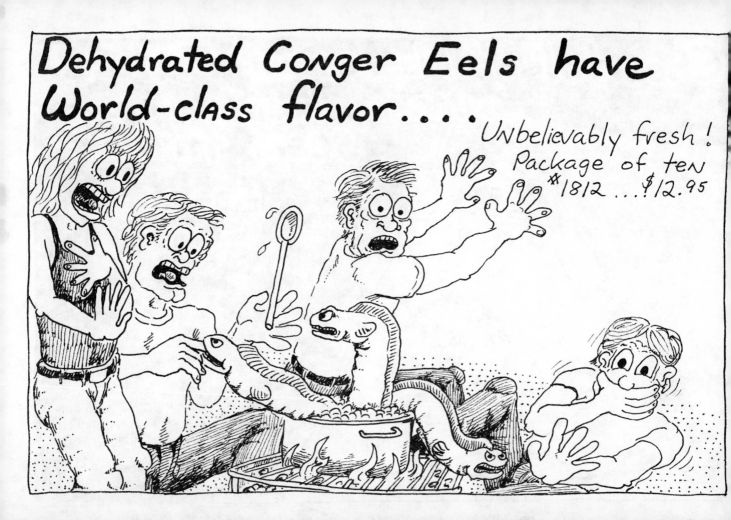

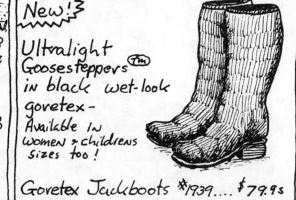

# Be a model for Winter's Early!
# Go on our catalogue road trip.....

Things get pretty boring up here in Antler, N. Dakota so each spring we load up the company car with beer, wine, and amateur teenage models and go for an exciting road trip to someplace exotic for catalogue photo sessions. Last year's trip to Juárez, Mexico will be long remembered by all our staff. Roach, our editor, should be getting out of jail just in time for this year's trip...

If you are age 16-25, female, attractive, and have a taste for white pills, wine, and group activities send us a recent photograph of yourself (bathing suit/full body shot, please). Respondents owning two or more major credit cards are given preferential treatment.

# Application for employment, catalogue photo/road trip

Name_____

Address_____

City/State_____

Phone_____

Today's Date_____

Date of Birth_____

Personal Reference_____

_____

Height_____ Weight_____

Hair Color_____ Eye Color_____

Female ☐ yes, ☐ No

Do you have in your possession any major credit cards? ☐ yes ☐ No

Do you find Nudity and lewd behavior objectionable?
☐ No      ☐ yes

Which of the following drugs

---

Would you most like to injest on any typical day?
☐ Quaaludes    ☐ LSD
☐ PCP ☐ Psycillocybin
☐ THC ☐ Ethyl Ether

Are you allergic to massive doses of penicillin?
☐ yes    ☐ No

Which of the following meals would you like to prepare for our staff on any typical day?
☐ Breakfast    ☐ Lunch
☐ Dinner ☐ Late Nite munchies

Would you object to sharing your sleeping bag with all our technical staff on

---

Attach a recent color photo of yourself here

a rotating basis?
☐ yes ☐ No

The Ultimate Shuttle?

# Running Ice
## Glacieryaking On The World's Mightiest Frozen River

Photographs of Epic
Proportion
By
Vernon Krugerrand,
Mike Ultimate,
And
Rebus Teegrip

On the edge of the Abyss.
Vernon perches dangerously near
the yawning bergschrund at the
head of Baltoro Glacier.....

# A Gaggle of Visionaries

**Vernon Krugerrand** - 49, of Big Stones, Indiana. Trip Leader Krugerrand is a long time veteran of the outdoor celebrity circuit. He dreams of a time when the world's people will throw away their nuclear weapons and take up marathon canoeing. "At that point I will become Supreme Emperor of Water World and then, by god, we'll <u>do</u> some paddling," Vernon claims. He recently completed a 100,000 mile canoe trip with his sidekick, Rebus Teegrip.

**Rebus Teegrip** - 32, of Flat Water, Ohio. Longtime friend and minion of Krugerrand, Rebus too wants to disarm the world and help Vernon rule the world community of boaters. "We could open up mandatory flatwater clinics worldwide and make some big BIG bucks." His upcoming book on Glacier running technique will feature over 150 color photographs of the world's most formidable glaciers.

**Mike Ultimate** - 50, of Karma Bay, Florida. Team metaphysician and master glacier yak designer, Mike led the recent renaissance in solo canoe thwart design that has revolutionized the sport of canoe waltzing. Ultimate has been acclaimed as the Fodor Dostoyevsky of dynamic thwart design. "I was a little nervous when Vernon asked me to design the Glacier yak prototype," Ultimate admits, "When you're talking glaciers you're talking about forces far beyond anything found on any regular river. Glaciers carved the Great Lakes and made Indiana look like a golf course...think what one could do to a 16' glacier yak!"

At ease in Kathmandu, Vernon, Mike, and Rebus review the torturous logistics of the upcoming helicopter shuttle that will take them and their 1,800 kgs. of equipment to the head of Baltoro Glacier.

Baltoro Glacier flows west from the base of Mt. Everest, the "Goddess Mother of the Earth". Baltoro is locally referred to as "Frozen Waters Flowing from the Nether Regions of Our Goddess Mother Earth".

"On the glacier the parameters of the possible expanded infinitely in all directions...." — Mike Ultimate

Rebus and Mike practice bracing as Vernon waves farewell to the helicopter shuttle crew. Little did the team suspect that this was to be their last contact with civilization for nearly thirty grueling days....

0900 - We begin the first boat descent of Baltoro Glacier. Bright sun and winds at 5-10 knots made for ideal glacier paddling. This was to be the only decent weather we experienced during the ordeal!

"Our maximum top speed was a 'glacial' 10 meters per hour," Krugerrand confessed," but at that pace you really develop a heightend awareness of the glacier."

Some beautiful ice formations....

Some other beautiful ice formations....

Day 3 — Mike suggests we practice our free-form glacieryak technique while ferrying to the opposite side of the glacier. This took two days. Rebus has begun to appear exhausted...

Day 5 — With a storm approaching, Vernon and Mike opt to push on while Rebus rests and brews up. They will rejoin 12 hours later, 150 meters down-glacier in the midst of a whiteout.

"Baltoro's capricious Nature did strange things to our minds... at one point Mike wandered naked into a total whiteout muttering about hull specs for a new solo glacieryak..." — Rebus Teegrip

"Tentbound for three days... ...bonds of friendship were assaulted by Nature herself." — Exerpt from Krugerrand's diary

frrraaaaap!

The long nights were excruciatingly dark and bitterly cold... the mere act of sleeping took on heroic proportions. To make things worse Ultimate was stricken with dysentery

"Day 11 — the weather cleared. It looked like a good omen...." — Vernon Krugerrand

Day 11 — Underway again (at last!) the team breaks camp and pushes on under improving conditions. After only a few hard-won meters Rebus looses control and falls over, unable to brace in the deep powder.......

"When Teegrip wiped out I began to sense a malignant force in the glacier itself.....It was trying to kill us." — Mike Ultimate

ho-yah
hey-yah
ho-yah...

Himself still stricken with dysentery, team metaphysician Ultimate administers emergency spiritual life support to hypothermic Rebus Teegrip.

"Just when it looked like our epic was over we reached the Khumbu Icefall..........Mike became obsessed with the 'extreme fragility of team karma'"

Concerned with the ever-weakening condition of Rebus, Vernon decides to carabiner the boats together with Teegrip in the middle position.

Krugerrand's carabiner safety system did prove to have a particular drawback.... Vernon suggests that future parties add a 150' 11mm climbing rope between boats and utilize a static snow anchor belay system!

"...my only regret is that I will never complete the 100,000 mile Ultimate Glacier Challenge.... Rebus has been unconcious for days and Mike ate our last package of croutons while I slept...all is lost."
— exerpt from Krugerrand's diary

Okay okay 800 dollars 'American' and not one penny more!

After three days trapped in the crevasse, unemployed sherpas wandering nearby answer their cries for help.

Vernon and Mike decide Rebus's condition warrants a sherpa assisted evacuation. $2,000.00 poorer, the two continue down the glacier, arriving at the foot of Baltoro eight days later. "The last mile was the longest." — Mike Ultimate

Back in Kathmandu Ultimate remarks, "Ours was an awesome achievment. I can only hope future generations of glacieryakers will fully appreciate the vast scope of our contribution to the sport."

Reunited the trio discuss their near-tragedy at Khumbu Icefall. Rebus still suffers with extensive frostbite, high altitude pulmonary edema, & mild dementia.

Vernon is already planning a new ultimate challenge-running Hawaiian lava flows. Mike has begun designing a radical new solo canoe with an asbestos/kevlar hull and thermocoupled thwarts...

...and it's back to the States to write about their daring exploits and to plan new challenges that will surely push the outer limits of glacieryaking still further!

# Tips for Glacieryakers...

☐ Use only A.G.A. approved glacieryaks and accessories.

☐ Make sure sponsorships by magazines and/or equipment manufacturers entail no awkward contract encumberances that place undue emphasis upon style _or_ successful completion of the expeditions stated objectives.

☐ When signing contracts with magazine and book publishers be sure to clarify that marathon glacieryakists construe "continuous" to mean actual time on glaciers _PLUS_ time spent off the glacier or between glaciers while on resupply or R.&R. missions. Resupply and/or R.&R. time should not exceed one month per three months per quarter.

☐ Maintain exclusivity on expedition photographs by written contract only. Even the best of friends can experience unpleasant lawsuits when custody of a camera or rolls of film are disputed by rival publishers or magazines.

# Resources -

Books, information...

☐ _Baltoro the Hard Way_ - Vernon Krugerrand, Sea Snail Press, Ontario, 1983 ....$19.95

☐ _Games Glacieryakists Play_ - Mike Ultimate, Guru Press, Karma Bay, 1983 ...... $18.95

☐ _The Ultimate Glacier Challenge_, _The True Story_ - Rebus Teegrip, Flatwater Press, New York, 1983 ............... $17.95

☐ _Solo on Baltoro_, _My Epic_ - M. Ultimate Guru Press, Karma Bay, 1983 ......$16.95

☐ _Medicine for Glacieryakers_ - R. Teegrip, Flatwater Press, New York, 1983...$15.95

# Equipment Manufacturers -

Tao Glaciercraft - The only A.G.A. approved manufacturer of glacieryaks and accessories. Designed by Master Designer and Thwart Aesthetician Mike Ultimate.. Tao Glacier-craft, Box 69, Karma Bay, Florida

# Organizations -

American Glacieryak Association (A.G.A.) P.O. Box 69 Karma Bay, Florida

Finally, a magazine for the paddler of the 80's... Victim Magazine!

An unsolicited testimonial...

Before I started reading Victim Magazine I couldn't achieve even a small entrapment... Now I'm having better and better entrapments! More often too! Can't wait 'till I find my "E-spot.".

VICTIM MAGAZINE

November 1984

$1.95

In this issue:

* Winter Pinning- New techniques to achieve cold water entrapment!

* The myth of Female Entrapment

* New hope for Fiberglass kayaks... All-nylon layup modifications....

* Tips from Tubers- How to get pinned <u>and</u> injured

* Coast Guard Approved P.F.D.'s - a threat to the sport?

* and much much more...

TECHNA

A Cut Above
the Others..

# Whitewater TV Guide

## TUESDAY

4:30 PM To 9:00 P.M.

7:30 (5) Peyson's Place - drama - John Boy sells an anthrax-ridden cow so he can buy a new racing K-1.

(7) People's Court - Cases involve a civil damage suit against T.V.A. and a kayak manufacturer.

(11)(2) Little House at the Takeout - drama - Pa (Michael Landon) takes a church group down the river and discovers Preacher Jim-Bob (John Ritter) is in reality Rev. Jim Jones of the People's Temple....

(48) Boating for Dollars - game show - Expert kayakers compete for trips and prizes by running a kayak simulator down a video river - the HBO-Bio. Host: Lee Majors

8:00 PM (7) Deliverance II (1983) - movie - Sequel to James Dickey's Deliverance - A vacationing team of mercenaries confront hostile mountain people while rafting a remote river gorge - Bobby: Mr. T, Lewis - George Peppard, Ed - Jamie Farr, Drew - John Denver

(2)(5) The Dukes of Gauley - A reformed call girl borrows General Lee to shuttle kayakers who turn out to be Bolivian cocaine smugglers. Repeat.

## Tonite

### Deliverance II
#### The Sequel

It's the A-Team vs. the Beverly Hillbillies on a deadly river of death!?
8:00
Don't Miss It!

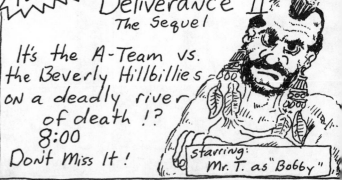

starring: Mr. T as "Bobby"

Bo-John Schneider, Luke-Tom Wombat, Daisy-Barbara Bach

(22) Rep Talk – talk show – Tonight's guest sales reps discuss buying trends in the plastic kayak market. Host-Tom Schlinkert (repeat)

(HBO) Tuesday Night Hacky Sack Playoffs – sports – Live from Chili Bar on the American River in California, The Denver DooDahs and the Seattle Sopors compete for Natl. Championship.

(1) Lava! – drama – J.R. tricks Sue Ellen into running an overloaded beer raft too far left in Lava Falls. Sue Ellen has a nasty swim. J.R.-Larry Hagman, Sue Ellen-Linda Gray, Pam-Victoria Principal

(PBS) Nova – science documentary – "Two-bladed Scientists" – Kayaking biologists search for endangered species in the Tuolome River.

8:30 (22) Whitewater Week in Review – new – A synopsis of river-related news items from the past week – Hosts-James Brolin, Barbara Bach

(2) Magnum K-I – Magnum (Tom Selleck) becomes involved with a gangster-moll enrolled in his kayak clinic. Co-starring Dolly Parton

Season Premiere

Is this any way to run a raft company?

THREE'S RAFT COMPANY 12 WTCT

9:00 P.M. to 10:30 P.M.

9:00 ② Survival of the Fittest - sports special - Famous climbers and kayakers dress up in suits and attempt to operate office machinery for big prizes. Host - Howard Cosell

㉒ S.M.A.S.H. - drama - Hawkeye and Trapper John meet a group of vacationing Swedish stewardesses who have lost their raft guide and are stranded in the Grand Canyon. It's loads of laughs for the "raftin' 4077th." Special Guest Star - Veronica Hamel as "Olga".

(PBS) The Iowa Paddling Repertory Company performs flatwater canoe ballet under the direction of conductor/composer Mike Ultimate

⑪ Slow and Dirty - Game show - Celebrity Bad Guys compete on a whitewater slalom course for money & prizes. Guests - Mr. T, Larry Hagman, Bruce Dern, Robert Mitchum.

⑦ The Love Raft - comedy - On tonite's episode the crew of the Love Raft take a champagne cruise in the Grand Canyon of the Stikine River in British Columbia.

The Hole Warrior - Mel Gibson plays a disgruntled kayaker who is fed up with boorish paddlers in his favorite surfing hole.
TONite! 10:00 PM
WBCT

9:30 ② - Fantasy Takeout - comedy - Tattoo helps a retired ad executive (Lorne Green) and his wife (Joan Rivers) rediscover their youth by paddling a canoe around the world. (Repeat)

㉒ Youghiogheny Five-O - drama - River rangers Steve and Dan-o investigate the theft of a beer cooler and stumble upon a bizarre cult of kayaking Rastafarians hiding in the state park.

10:00 - ②⑦ The Hole Warrior - movie - Angry kayaker goes after a group of rude paddlers on Tennessee's Ocoee river.

⑪ Charlie's Shuttle Bunnies - drama - Jill gets hopelessly lost in the shuttle bus and is bitten by a rabid skunk when she attempts to give it first aid.

㉒ Pine Creek Blues - Renko and Bobby are taken hostage by hostile drug smugglers during a river rescue. Faye gives Frank an ultimatum about solo paddling. Joyce Davenport departs for Chile's Bio-Bio for an interview for raft guide.

⑤ Diff'rent Strokes - Gary Coleman and his special guest Eddie Murphy discuss the pros & cons of the cross-draw, bow pry, and reverse sweep.

At the movie house it's 9 o'clock..
EXIT
EXIT
Beep!
Beep!
Beep!
Beep!
Beep!
Beep!
Beep!
Beep!
Beep!
Beep
Beep!
Beep!
Beep!
Beep!
Beep!
Beep!
BEEP!
Beep!
Beep!
Beep!
Beep!
Beep!
Beep!

Hair Gondolier

# Three Grab Loop Modifications You Can Do...

## ① Simple breakaway loop system-

cut grab loop and resecure with rubber cement.

## ② The Infinite grab loop...

200' open spool of 3/8" polypro. rope

## ③ Breakaway Stern

Ach!

① Obtain one (1) end section of a boat similar to yours. This can be accomplished in a few seconds with a small chainsaw or folding camp saw at any take-out or boater campground.

② Lightly hammer over stern of your boat.

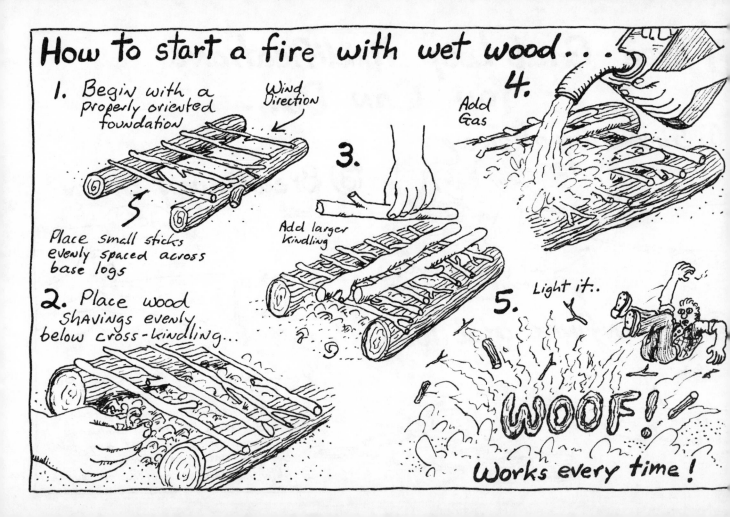

The Ultimate Playboat ?

# The River Tale...

**Did I tell you guys about running Wind Creek Gorge this Spring?**

**Not yet....**

**Well, it rained solid for a week before so it was smokin'. Don called me up and said he'd been scouting it and it was incredible! Wow! A first run in this awesome canyon! I had to... thought "what the... only chance... talking about dam... or 6 years. So I sai... SNOWING...**

**Sure.......**
**Hey, didja hear my new tape of the Bush Tetras yet?**

**Hand me a beer, would you?**
**...ing it up "Sure."**

**No. Play it, I hear they're bizarre...**

**t saw them up w in D.C. last c week.... sounded m like Lawrence i Welk on P.C.P... ble that ...uld have des... Not to m...ntion that i... and still snowing li... weaving a divers w... was stil freezing my... then we got to the the gor...e. It necks... 250 feet ...er mile or s...**

**put in w... Don nearly lost was Class 5 for lipped and rolle ...iss this terminal**

**Really!** ...eep ...is boat ...about 2 ...up just ...ock jum... ...t th...

**We got to see the Insect Surfers last time we went to D.C. ... pass that over this way, Bogart... Anyhow, they played at about 160 decibels..**

**I heard they w were great. w How was the c audience? D in case**

**I couldn't see ru...ing it ...ejackets and at east boat. I tried it f...st with in the eddy hold ...iust somebody flipped**

**Pretty cool.... a little too hip for my taste...**

Was b[eg]inning to get p... but at this point we cou... had to run it or freeze... pretty and shape but...

There was this one guy with a green mohawk who kept puking on people.....

Lots of weirdos in D.C.. Possibly the proximity to the White House...

twelve ... by a gigantic ... d an underc[urrent] ... just mi[ssed] ... hydralic rock, but...

swim ... but the curren... got h[im] and his boat... built [on] five and tried to dec[ide] if we should... continue. It was get[ting] dark ... was getting ... [e]ven worse.. No food anyw[a]y so we run it or die... in the "Go for it!" I ... before...

No doubt. Nice clubs though...

They also get more than their fair share of beautiful foxes...

Yeah...last time I met this woman who was absolutely...

God, how bizarre. Did she really *do* that? Really?

e fifth drop w... ut we couldn'[t] flip in the...

s the ... carry...

hole ... ut I surfed it and ... [f]inally I endere[d] in ti[m]e for the last tw[e]lv[e] feet or highe[r]...

No joke. Then we went back out to a different club and got real drunk...

Unreal. That kinda stuff never happens to me. If the woman's not a boater I don't know what to say...

really terminal h[o]le so little seam betw[e]en the drolics. I hit it r[i]ght on off the drop and into the eddy. [We] great first [r]... made [i]t!

ISN'T THAT INCREDIBLE!

Oh yeah?

What?

Huh?

# S & M River Supplies

# Supplies

# 1984 Catalogue

Ride the Wild Psyche!
It's cosmic!
It's the latest California craze!
Ommmmmm......
In S&M's New Hypalon Sensory Deprivation Tank
Whether you're a Taurus or an Aquarian or anything in between, you'll love the relaxing sensation of floating big rapids in a mystical trance!
Hypalon Sens/Dep Tank......$2695.00
Epsom Salt.....$2.00 lb.

# S&M's Body Croakie....

## The ultimate in passive upper-body restraint!

Available in red, yellow, black and blue

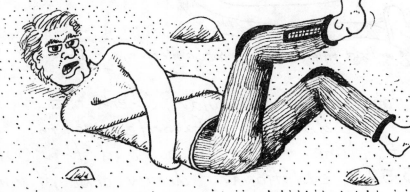

Coming soon: Wrist and ankle croakies....

# Introducing the B-52 Bomber Kayak!

Designed by America's foremost authority on existential boat design, W. Nealy...

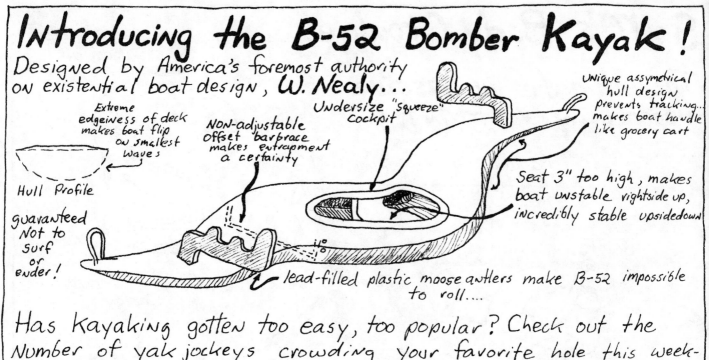

**Unique assymetical hull design prevents tracking... makes boat handle like grocery cart**

**Undersize "squeeze" Cockpit**

**Extreme edgeiness of deck makes boat flip on smallest waves**

**NON-adjustable offset barbrace makes entrapment a certainty**

**Hull Profile**

**guaranteed Not to surf or ender!**

**Seat 3" too high, makes boat unstable rightside up, incredibly stable upsidedown**

**lead-filled plastic moose antlers make B-52 impossible to roll....**

Has kayaking gotten too easy, too popular? Check out the Number of yak jockeys crowding your favorite hole this weekend! Don't you think it's time to spread out and thin out our ranks? Nealy's B-52's evolutionary design concept will turn easy CLASS I & II rapids into deadly adrenaline-pumping Class VI rapids. Punch the envelope with a B-52 Bomber!

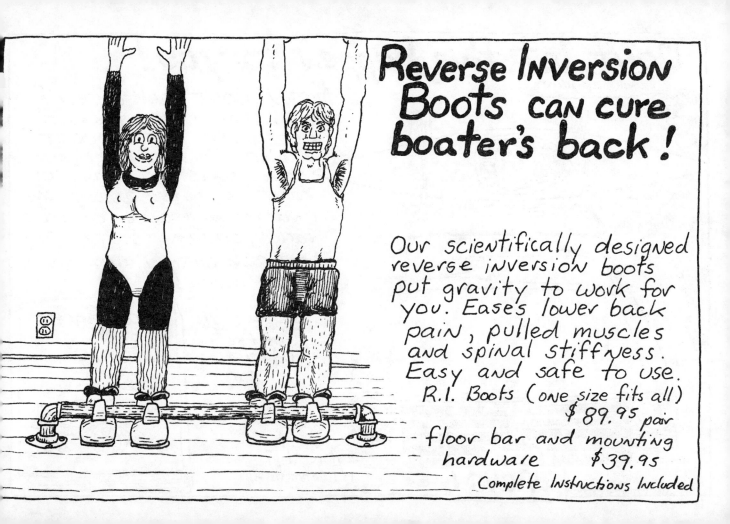

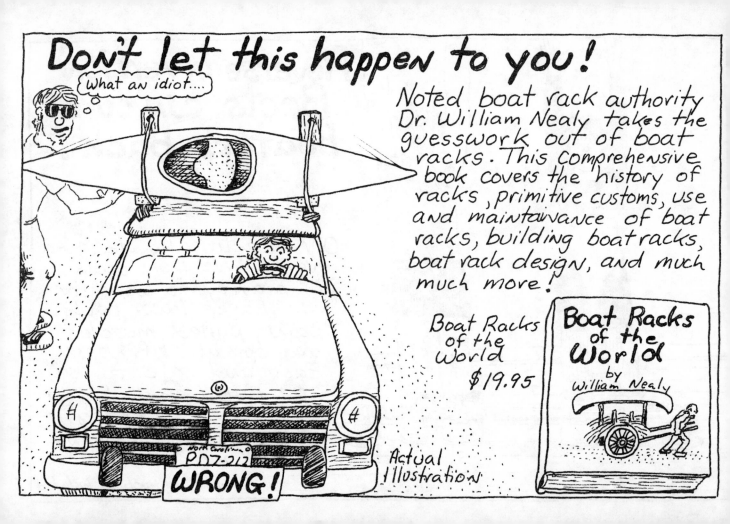

## The S&M Campfire Songbook...

### My Boat* (Nealy/Schlinkert/Wallace)

I've got sunshine on a cloudy day....
When it's cold outside I've got the
   month of May....
(Chorus) I guess you'll say what can
   make me feel this way....
my boat...... my boat...... my boat..........
talkin' 'bout my boat......... my boat!
   ooooooo ooooooooooo (fade)
Moves so fast in the water the
fish envy me......
I'm surfing bigger waves, baby,
than old Waikiki.....
           (Chorus)
I don't need no duct tape, got
no busted seams.....
She's made of Kevlar......

*Sung to the tune of "My Girl"-Temptations

### The kayak of my dreams...
        (Chorus)
I've got dry feet on a rainy day....
In my cockpit it's the month of May..
It's such a dry boat
........ my boat! (fade out)
©1983- Wet White Boys Music, Inc.

---

Plus much much more!
Here's what else you get.....
"Death Raft!"                "My Wave!"
            "We gotta get out of
"Hole Hog" "Punch Out    this hole"
           At Chili Bar"    "Proud
                             C-boat"
"Gimmie Kevlar"

                             "Knees of
                              Stone"
"I did it my way"              "Tequila!"

The S&M Campfire Songbook (160 pp)
shipping included.............$6.95

# The Hunky Dory...

This rugged 18' dory comes equipped with the famous Hungarian SA-677X ground-to-air radar-guided missle system. Extremely effective against tour helicopters and airborne kayaks.

Only $124,265.95 each

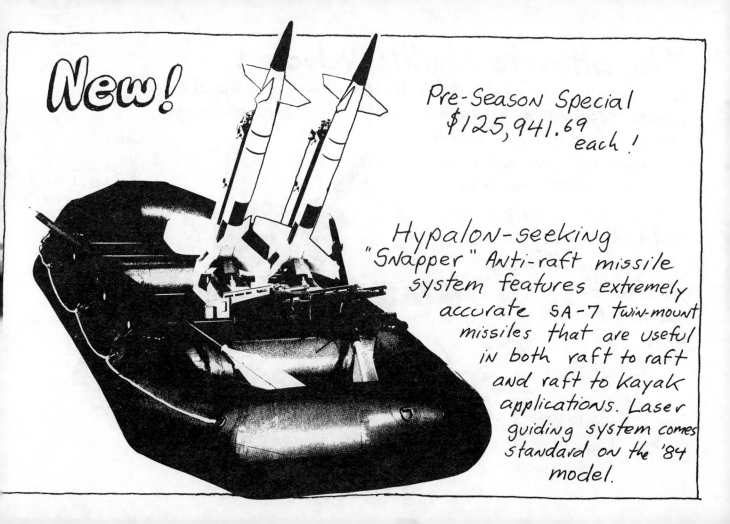

# The ultimate shuttle vehicle?

We think so. The 1984 M-113 Armored Personel Carrier comes standard equipped with the extraordinary 20 m.m. Vulcan A.A. electric cannon. Imagine what the Vulcan's 6000 rounds per minute cyclic rate could do to a slow-moving Winnebago Chieftan full of touroid leafers from Florida!

ONLY

$ 985,629.⁰⁰ each

Goes Anywhere,
Anytime!

# The New River "Sweep" Raft

We think you'll find our turret mounted 4" and 6" howitzers are a real dynamic duo! Turret extension on the 6" gun allows for a full 360° of coverage. With the optional Falcon 4-C wire-guided missile you'll literally "rule the standing waves"!
Only $275,450.³⁹

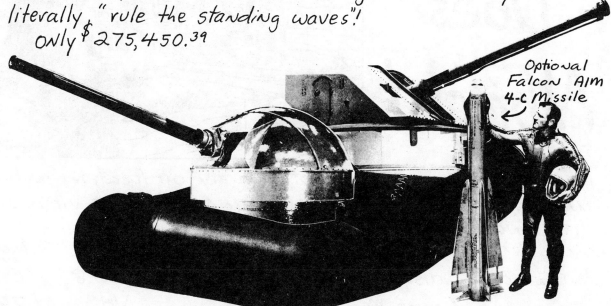

Optional Falcon AIM 4-C Missile

# Debbie Does Albright

The ultimate whitewater training film

Shot entirely on location in the mountains of West Virginia

Available in: 8mm $39.95
Super 8 $59.95
VHS $79.95

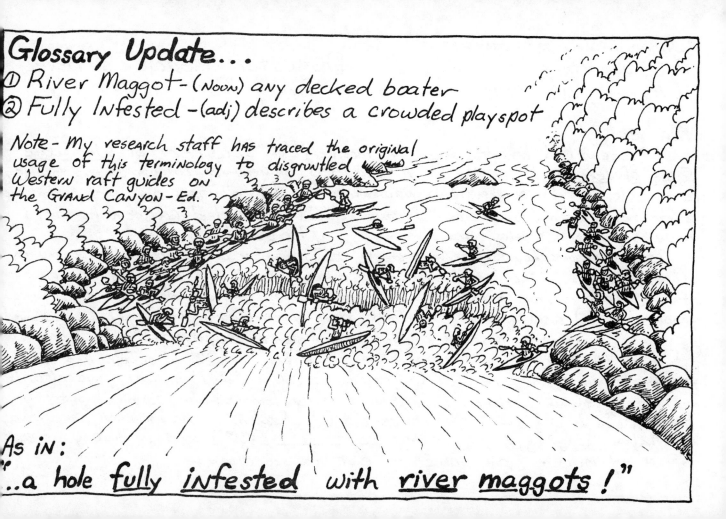

William Nealy / S&m Products
Rt 3, Box 450
Hillsborough, N.C. 27278

Disgusted Readers - Here's a handy form letter! ↙

Mr. Nealy;
    I recently (bought, acquired, received [circle one]) a copy of _Whitewater Tales of Terror_. It is the most (tasteless, sickening, disgusting, deplorable, awful, depraved, reprehensible, nauseating [circle one]) collection of (sociopathic, sic demented, offensive, onerous, obnoxious [circle one]) so-called cartoon humor I have seen in (weeks, years, recently, my life [circle one]).
    As a (responsible, respected, revered [circle one]) member of the paddling community, I (was, am [circle one]) (shocked, sickened, disturbed, saddened [circle one]) by your depiction of (paddlers, women boaters, equipment manufactures, boat designers, rafters, mountain people [circle one]) as (inferior, mindless, drug-crazed, egotistical, other_____ [circle one]) (zombies, sex-objects, morons, cretins, automatons, sex perverts [circle one])!
    It is too bad a few (irresponsible, deranged, sick [circle one]) people like you are trying to ruin the sport of (canoeing, kayaking [circle one]) for everyone else. If you really think paddlers are (stupid, silly, lemming-like, cosmically superfluous, boring, [circle one]) why don't you take up (scubadiving, hanggliding, skydiving, triathalon, jogging, skiing, other_____ [circle one]) and inflict your poor sense of humor on someone else for a change.

(Next page →)

For your information, there are many people involved in whitewater sports who are not brain-damaged habitual drug-abusers like yourself. I myself am (a, an [Circle one]) (expert canoeist, expert kayaker, certified canoe instructor, canoe livery owner, outfitter, boat designer, equipment manufacturer, [Circle one]) with many years of experience both on and off rivers and I fail to see the humor in any of your material.

Why don't you (grow up, quit drawing, f**k off [Circle one]))!

Yours,

P.S.- (I want my money back!)
(I'm suing you for libel!) [Circle one]

## Other Menasha Ridge Press Guidebooks

Kayaks to Hell
by William Nealy

Whitewater Home Companion, Southeastern Rivers,
  Volume I, William Nealy

Whitewater Home Companion, Southeastern Rivers,
  Volume II, William Nealy

Nantahala River Flip Map, Ron Rathnow

Ocoee River Flip Map, Ron Rathnow

Carolina Whitewater: A Canoeist's Guide to the
  Western Carolinas, Bob Benner

Wildwater West Virginia, Volume I, The Northern
  Streams, Paul Davidson and Ward Eister, with
  Dirk Davidson

Wildwater West Virginia, Volume II, The Southern
  Streams, Paul Davidson and Ward Eister, with
  Dirk Davidson

Shipwrecks: Diving the Graveyard of the Atlantic,
  Roderick Farb

Smoky Mountains Trout Fishing Guide, Don Kirk

A Fishing Guide to Kentucky's Major Lakes, Arthur B.
  Lander, Jr.

A Canoeing and Kayaking Guide to the Streams of
  Florida, Volume I, North Central Peninsula and
  Panhandle, Elizabeth F. Carter and John L. Pearce

Appalachian Whitewater, Volume I, The Southern
  Mountains, Bob Sehlinger, Don Otey, Bob Benner,
  William Nealy, and Bob Lantz

Northern Georgia Canoeing, Bob Sehlinger and
  Don Otey

Southern Georgia Canoeing, Bob Sehlinger and
  Don Otey

A Canoeing and Kayaking Guide to the Streams of
  Ohio, Volume I, Richard Combs and
  Stephen E. Gillen

A Canoeing and Kayaking Guide to the Streams of
  Ohio, Volume II, Richard Combs and
  Stephen E. Gillen

*A Canoeing and Kayaking Guide to the Streams of Kentucky,* Bob Sehlinger

*A Canoeing and Kayaking Guide to the Streams of Tennessee, Volume I,* Bob Sehlinger and Bob Lantz

*A Canoeing and Kayaking Guide to the Streams of Tennessee, Volume II,* Bob Sehlinger and Bob Lantz

*Boat Builder's Manual,* Charles Walbridge, editor

*A Fishing Guide to the Streams of Kentucky,* Arthur B. Lander, Jr.

*A Guide to the Backpacking and Day-Hiking Trails of Kentucky,* Arthur B. Lander, Jr.

*A Guide to Kentucky Outdoors,* Arthur B. Lander, Jr.